EDGE BOOKS

THE KIDS' GUIDE TO

Jumping Rope

BY SHERI BELL-REHWOLDT

Consultant:

Lisa Brown

Member, USA Jump Rope and Saltare

CAPSTONE PRESS
a capstone imprint

Edge Books are published by Capstone Press,
151 Good Counsel Drive, P.O. Box 669, Mankato, Minnesota 56002.
www.capstonepub.com

 Books published by Capstone Press are manufactured with paper
containing at least 10 percent post-consumer waste.

Library of Congress Cataloging-in-Publication Data
Bell-Rehwoldt, Sheri.
  The kids' guide to jumping rope / by Sheri Bell-Rehwoldt.
    p. cm. — (Edge books. Kids' guides)
  Includes bibliographical references and index.
  Summary: "Describes the sport of jumping rope, including how-to information
on jumps and tricks"—Provided by publisher.
  ISBN 978-1-4296-5443-2 (library binding)
  1. Rope skipping—Juvenile literature. I. Title. II. Series.
  GV498.B45 2011
  796.2—dc22   2010035018

Editorial Credits

Angie Kaelberer, editor; Kyle Grenz, designer, Eric Gohl, media researcher;
    Eric Manske, production specialist

Photo Credits

All images from Capstone Press/Karon Dubke, except:
Alamy/The Art Gallery Collection, 22
AP Images/PictureGroup/Mark Davis, 17, 29
Courtesy of Tahira Reid, 27 (bottom)
Getty Images/Museum of the City of New York/Jacob A. Riis, 5
iStockphoto/Tommi Laurila (jump rope), 5, 7, 29
Shutterstock/nito, cover

Printed in the United States of America in Stevens Point, Wisconsin.
092010   005934WZS11

TABLE OF CONTENTS

THE WHOLE WORLD JUMPS

You probably chose this book because jumping rope looks like fun. Well, you're right!

Jumping rope is simple to learn and also offers much variety. You can do it on your own. Or you can jump with a friend or even the whole neighborhood. The fun and challenges ahead depend only upon the number of ropes and the skills of the jumpers.

Remember that the sky is the limit to what you can do when you begin jumping rope. Some kids who start out jumping in their garage end up on amateur jump teams that compete for prizes. A handful of jumpers have even become professionals. These jumpers earn money for their signature style and speed.

amateur—an athlete who competes without being paid
professional—an athlete who receives money for competing

In the past, clothing styles sometimes determined who jumped rope. In the 1700s, girls couldn't jump rope because of their long skirts. So boys took over the sport. But when skirts shortened in the 1800s, girls grabbed their ropes.

JUMPING THROUGH HISTORY

Children have jumped rope for thousands of years. They used whatever materials they had available. Archaeologists have uncovered ancient Greek vases showing children jumping over vines. Years ago, kids in Hungary used jump ropes made of braided straw. Those in New Zealand jumped thin leather ropes used to tie up cows. For many years, British and American kids used window sash cords and telephone wire. Cloth, leather, and plastic jump ropes are all popular today.

The sport requires only one tool—a rope. But you'll need to carefully choose that rope based on the type of jumping you do. Lengths vary depending on whether you're jumping alone or in a group. Too long, and the rope will be hard to swing. Too short, and you'll have to hunch over to jump—and will likely trip!

CLOTH ROPE

PLASTIC ROPE

BEADED ROPE

The material the rope is made of is also important. Beginners often choose lightweight cloth ropes. These ropes don't sting much when they hit you, which will happen as you learn.

Many jumpers like beaded plastic ropes for their speed, control, and precision. Plus the rope's distinctive click makes setting a jumping rhythm easy. But plastic ropes are heavier and take more effort to turn than cloth ropes.

precision—accuracy or exactness

MEASURE TWICE

To jump by yourself, measure the rope to your height. The general rule for measuring is to stand on the middle of the rope. The rope length is perfect when the ends of the rope or rope handles reach your armpits. If you're jumping with a friend, the rope should reach the armpits of the taller jumper.

Fun Fact:

In a poll taken by a jump rope company, 649 jumpers picked their favorite ropes:

Beaded ropes (46%, 297 Votes)

Plastic/speed ropes (27%, 177 Votes)

Cloth ropes (16%, 107 Votes)

Cable/Wire ropes (11%, 68 Votes)

Where you jump also matters. Outdoor jumpers need heavier ropes that stand up to the wind. Plastic ropes are also good for outdoors because they are water-resistant.

Jumping puts stress on your entire body, but especially your feet. The best place to jump is on a wooden floor with some spring to it, such as a gym floor. Rubber floors or sports mats also provide good support. If you have to jump on a road or sidewalk, wear good-quality athletic shoes. You will need the padding in the shoes to absorb the shock of your jumping. But avoid shoes that have thick knobs on the soles. They'll likely snag and catch on the rope. And don't jump on thick foam mats. They take the bounce out of your landing, putting even more pressure on your legs. Never jump in bare feet or sandals. Doing that can hurt your feet and ankles.

WARM UP

Before jumping, do at least five minutes of jumping jacks, knee lifts, and other leg exercises like skipping or jumping on one or both feet. These activities will pump your blood and warm up your muscles. After a bit of warming up, be sure to stretch out your calves, quadriceps, and hamstrings. And don't forget to stretch your arm, shoulder, and neck muscles. You don't have to spend a lot of time stretching. Just do it until you feel your muscles loosen up.

Fun Fact:

According to the Jump Rope Institute, jumping 120 revolutions per minute for 10 minutes provides the same benefits as jogging 30 minutes or playing two sets of tennis.

BOTTOMS UP

Keep a water bottle close by to stay hydrated. Water makes up about 60 percent of your body and 70 percent of your brain. Lose too much water through sweating and both will fizzle long before your enthusiasm does.

JUMPING SOLO

Jumping rope is the perfect cure for boredom. Learn the following jumps, combine them into routines, and you'll be ready for the big time.

Keep your elbows close to your body and your arms bent as you swing the rope. Start each new trick with the same foot. Practice without the rope to master the steps.

BASIC JUMPS

BASIC JUMP: Jump over the rope as you swing it in front of you, bouncing on the balls of both feet. Once you can do this easily, try swinging the rope backward instead of forward.

ALTERNATE FEET: Jump over the rope using first one foot, then the other. This jump is twice as fast as the basic jump.

TOE TAP: Jump and touch your toe to the ground behind you. Keep your weight on your other foot. Switch feet and touch the other toe to the ground.

HEEL TAP: Jump and touch your heel to the ground in front of you. Keep your weight on your other foot. Switch feet and touch the other heel to the ground.

SIDE SWING: Bring your hands together along the right side of your body as you twirl the rope. Move your left hand to your left side and open the rope to do a basic jump. Move both hands to the left and twirl the rope.

STRADDLE: Do a jumping jack with your feet. Open your legs with one jump and land with them about 1 foot (0.3 meter) apart. Bring your legs back together with the next jump.

CROSS STRADDLE: Like the Straddle, open your legs with the first jump, but cross them on the next jump.

SCISSORS: Jump, putting one foot forward and the other back. Switch feet with every jump.

SKIER: Jump 4 to 6 inches (10 to 15 centimeters) to the right in a basic jump, keeping your feet together. Then jump 4 to 6 inches to the left in a basic jump.

BELL: Jump 4 to 6 inches (10 to 15 centimeters) forward and then back in a basic jump. Keep your feet together.

DOUBLE UNDER: Jump a bit higher than you usually do, swinging the rope under your feet twice before doing a basic jump.

TRIPLE UNDER: This move is much like a Double Under. You swing the rope under your feet three times before doing a basic jump.

CAN-CAN: Lift your right knee as you jump on your left foot. Follow that by a jump with both feet on ground. Jump again on your left foot as you kick your right leg in front of you. Repeat with your other leg.

Jumping alone is satisfying, but jumping with friends is even better. Group jumping with a long rope requires mastering the entrance and exit. And you must fine-tune your coordination skills if you want to try synchronized jumping. This is when two jumpers share the same rope.

IN AND OUT

A single rope can be turned two ways. If the rope hits the ground and moves away from you, it's called a "front door." If the rope moves toward you, it's a "back door." Using the front door is the easiest way to jump in and out.

FRONT DOOR ENTRANCE

TO ENTER:

Front door entrance: Stand next to the turner's shoulder. After the rope hits the ground and moves away, jump into the center of the rope. Jump when the rope comes back around.

Back door entrance: When the rope reaches its full height, quickly run in. Take an immediate jump to clear the rope as it comes down.

BACK DOOR ENTRANCE

TO EXIT:

Finish your jump, then take another jump that turns you toward a turner. Step out quickly, aiming for the turner's shoulder.

TANDEM TRICKS

When you and one or more friends jump together with the same rope, you're jumping in unison. It takes skill. Though only one of you turns the rope, you both jump!

SHORT ROPE INSIDE A LONG ROPE

This trick calls for two turners and one or more jumpers.

0 The jumper enters the rope carrying the short rope. For this trick, the jumper's rope may be shorter than usual.

2 The jumper jumps the short rope in rhythm with the long rope. The turners make sure that the long rope is going high over the jumper's head.

3 The jumper stops jumping the short rope and takes a few jumps over the long rope before exiting.

4 For more fun, add another jumper!

THE TRAVELER

0 You'll need five jumpers and one rope that is long enough for the tallest jumper.

2 Line up four jumpers side-by-side. You'll turn the rope.

3 Stand behind the line, directly behind the first person. As you swing the rope, cue the first person. Both of you will jump together. Jump precisely to keep the rope going.

4 Cue the first person when you're ready to move down the line. The first person stops jumping as you move on to the second person. But the rope does not stop.

5 After traveling the entire line, work your way back to the first person. The jumpers in line can double up so that three of you jump together.

6 With practice and a long enough rope, all five of you might manage to jump together!

JUMPING IN RHYME

New jumping rhymes are being thought up all the time. Some rhymes are created to count the number of jumps a jumper makes before messing up. Other rhymes give jumpers instructions of tricks to do as they jump. These two rhymes are examples of counting and trick rhymes:

Cinderella, dressed in yella,
Went upstairs to kiss a fella,
Made a mistake and kissed a snake,
How many doctors will it take?
1, 2, 3, 4, etc.

Not last night, but the night before
Twenty-four robbers came a-knocking at my door
As I ran out (jump out), they ran in (Jump back in.)
Hit me over the head with a rolling pin!
(Pretend to hit self on head.)
Asked them what they wanted, this is what they said:
Spanish dancers, do the splits (Do splits.)
Spanish dancers, give a high kick (Kick.)
Spanish dancers, turn around (Turn around.)
Spanish dancers, touch the ground (Touch the ground.)
Spanish dancers, get out of town! (Jump out.)

Not all rhymes contain rhyming words. Many rhymes are just silly phrases designed to add more fun to the game. But some rhymes are taken from stories or actual events. The story about President George Washington chopping down a cherry tree led to this rhyme:

George Washington
never told a lie.
Until he ran around the corner
and stole a cherry pie.
How many cherries were in that pie?
1, 2, 3, 4, etc.

When you're jumping solo, you need to think only of yourself. But when you jump in groups, you must know how to turn the rope for others. To become a great turner, here are some useful tips.

PREPPING THE ROPES

Each turner takes an end of the rope, standing far enough apart that the rope is almost taut. Standing with their legs shoulder-width apart, they hold the rope ends tightly at about waist height. They are careful not to place their thumbs inside their fists. And they don't wrap the ropes around their hands. Doing either can cause injury.

Fun Fact:

There are two basic jumping cadences—the march and the bounce. The bounce is used for basic jumping. You bounce up and down on the balls of your feet. To march, raise your knees high. This allows you to jump with speed. In both styles, jumpers keep their feet and ankles close together.

KEEPING THINGS STRAIGHT

Turners keep their backs straight. If they lean into the rope, the rope goes slack. If they lean backward, the rope lifts off the floor. When turning a single rope, turners keep their thumbs on top of the rope and their wrists locked. They move only their lower arms.

When using two ropes, turners circle their hands between their nose and waist. They turn the ropes inward. Their left hands turn clockwise, and their right hands turn counter-clockwise. They don't cross the middle of their body with their hands. Doing this collapses the ropes.

ADJUST THE SPEED

For some jumps and tricks, turners need to either slow down or speed up the rope. To slow the rope, turners fully extend their arms to make the circles larger and slower. To speed the rope, they bring their arms closer to their bodies, making smaller and faster circles.

Double Dutch It

Double Dutch is a team sport. The word "double" refers to the setup of two ropes, two turners, and one or more jumpers. Double Dutch uses basic jumping skills as well as gymnastic and dance moves.

Ancient Egyptian and Chinese rope makers may be responsible for the Double Dutch jumping style. To make the ropes, the workers wrapped hemp around their waists in a twisting motion. Their helpers had to quickly jump over the ropes so they wouldn't trip. Eventually the jumping became a game for the workers and spread to other countries.

settlers arrived in what is now New York City in the 1600s, they brought the game with them. It became known as "Double Dutch."

Interest in Double Dutch decreased in the 1950s. But it enjoyed a comeback in 1973. That year, New York City police officers David Walker and Ulysses Williams organized the first Double Dutch tournament for inner-city kids.

hemp—plant fibers used to make rope

DOUBLE DUTCH TURNING

The most important part of Double Dutch is the turning.

1 You and the other turner should stand far enough apart to hold the rope taut between you.

2 Turn the ropes in small circles between your nose and waist. Your left hand turns clockwise, and your right hand turns counter-clockwise.

3 Be careful not to cross the middle of your body with your hands. This will cause the rope to collapse.

4 Walk toward each other until the rope barely touches the ground.

MASTER THE DOORWAYS

Once the turners are ready, it's time to show off your fancy tricks. But to do that, you'll need to get in and out of the ropes. Here's how:

TO ENTER:

1 Stand next to one rope turner's shoulder, facing the other turner.

2 Because there are two ropes turning in opposite directions, you have both front and back doors to enter! When the back rope, which is the one farthest from you, touches the ground, enter with a big step and jump.

TO EXIT:

1 Face a turner.

2 Jump slightly forward toward the turner.

3 As you jump out, aim for the turner's shoulder.

Tricks and Tips

0 Start out using ropes of different colors to keep them straight in your mind.

2 Start out with solo jumps, such as Toe Tap, Straddle, Skier, Bell, and Can-Can.

3 Add a partner. Try unison jumps, turns, and dance steps.

4 Add a single rope, jumping with it and the two Double Dutch ropes. Make sure you jump to

5 Add basic gymnastics moves such as handstands or cartwheels. Be careful—these are expert moves!

6 If you like to jump fast, use the marching step to get the turners really whipping those ropes.

AN AMAZING INVENTION

Tahira Reid loved jumping rope in elementary school. In third grade she came up with an idea for a rope turning machine for a school contest. In 1997 Reid was taking an engineering design class at Rensselaer Polytechnic Institute in New York. She decided to design and build the automatic rope turning machine as a class project. In 2000 Reid demonstrated the machine on the *The Today Show*. She also has a patent for her invention.

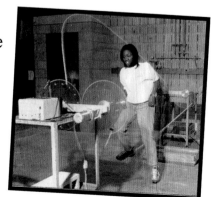

JUMP TO IT

Once you've mastered jumping rope, you might want to learn more about the sport. A great group to get involved with is USA Jump Rope (USAJR). USAJR offers camps, workshops, and a tournament series that leads to a national tournament held each year. The camps are usually three to five days long and are designed to teach both knowledge and skill. The single-day workshops help jumpers improve their skills. In the tournament series, events include speed, freestyle, and Double Dutch jumping.

JUMPING CLUBS

You can also check with your school to see if it has or plans to start a jump rope club. If not, you can start one yourself!

JUMPING ON MTV

Saltare is a group of Double Dutch jumpers from Raleigh, North Carolina. In 2010 this six-member team was part of Season 5 of the MTV show *America's Best Dance Crew.* In Spanish, Saltare means "to jump," which the team loves to do! Saltare didn't make it to the finals of the show, but the team introduced many people to competitive jumping.

Many schools participate in the American Heart Association's Jump Rope for Heart program. Students jump to raise money for other kids who have medical problems with their hearts.

Glossary

amateur (A-muh-chuhr)—an athlete who participates in a sport without being paid

cadence (KAY-duhnss)—a rhythmic flow of sounds or movements

freestyle (FREE-styl)—a type of competitive jumping that includes timed, judged routines

hemp (HEMP)—a plant whose fibers are used to make rope and sacks

patent (PAT-uhnt)—a legal document that gives an inventor the right to make, use, or sell an invention for a set number of years

precision (pri-SIH-shuhn)—accuracy or exactness

professional (pruh-FESH-uh-nuhl)—a person who receives money for taking part in a sport or activity

taut (TAWT)—something that is pulled tight and straight

unison (YOO-nuh-suhn)—when two or more people do or say the same thing at the same time

READ MORE

Bailey, Guy. *The Ultimate Playground and Recess Game Book*. Camas, Wash.: Educators Press, 2001.

Rau, Dana Meachen. *Jump Rope*. Games Around the World. Minneapolis: Compass Point Books, 2005.

Wise, Debra. *Great Big Book of Children's Games: Over 450 Indoor and Outdoor Games for Kids*. New York: McGraw-Hill, 2003.

INTERNET SITES

FactHound offers a safe, fun way to find Internet sites related to this book. All of the sites on FactHound have been researched by our staff.

Here's all you do:

Visit *www.facthound.com*

Type in this code: 9781429654432

 **Super-cool stuff!** Check out projects, games and lots more at **www.capstonekids.com**

INDEX